SCHOLASTIC

English Practice for

Year 5

Ages 9–10

This book belongs to:

SCHOLASTIC

English Year 5, Book 1

Book End, Range Road, Witney, Oxfordshire, OX29 0YD
www.scholastic.co.uk

2 3 4 5 6 7 8 9   6 7 8 9 0 1 2 3

British Library Cataloguing-in-Publication Data
A catalogue record for this book is available from the British Library.

ISBN 978-1407-14201-2
Printed in Italy by STIGE - Turin

Editorial
Rachel Morgan, Melissa Somers, Sarah Sodhi and Catherine Baker

Design
Scholastic Design Team: Neil Salt, Nicolle Thomas
and Oxford Designers & Illustrators Ltd

Cover Design
Neil Salt

Illustration
Thomas Giovanis

Acknowledgements
The publishers gratefully acknowledge permission to reproduce the following copyright material: **Kevin Crossley-Holland** for the use of an extract from *Room for one more* by Kevin Crossley-Holland © 1998, Kevin Crossley-Holland (1998, Oxford University Press). **Kit Wright** for the use of 'My dad, your dad' by Kit Wright from *Rabbiting On* by Kit Wright © 1978, Kit Wright (1978, Collins). **Her Majesty's Stationery Office** for the use of an extract from *What you need to know about driving licences* (D100) produced by the DVLA © 2005, Crown copyright Crown copyright material is reproduced with the permission of the Controller of HMSO and the Queen's Printer for Scotland. **The Society of Authors** for the use of 'Hints on Pronunciation for Foreigners' by George Bernard Shaw. Poem © 1965, George Bernard Shaw (1965, Sunday Times Letters). Every effort has been made to trace copyright holders for the works reproduced in this book, and the publishers apologise for any inadvertent omissions.

Contents

Why buy this book?

This series has been designed to support the introduction of the new National Curriculum in schools in England. The new curriculum is more challenging in English and includes the requirement for children's understanding to be secure before moving on. These practice books will help your child practise all of the skills they will learn at school, including some topics they might not have encountered previously.

How to use this book

- The content is divided into National Curriculum topics (for example, Spelling, Grammar, Comprehension and so on). Find out what your child is doing in school and dip into the relevant practice activities as required.
- Let your child know you are sharing the activities and support if necessary using the helpful quick tips at the top of most pages.
- Keep the working time short and come back to an activity if your child finds it too difficult. Ask your child to note any areas of difficulty. Don't worry if your child does not 'get' a concept first time, as children learn at different rates and content is likely to be covered throughout the school year.
- Check your child's answers using the answers section at the end of this book.
- Give lots of encouragement and tick off the progress chart as your child completes each chapter.

How to use the book

This is the title of the activity.

This tells you which topic you're working on.

Letters in slashes (like this) tell you it's the sound and not the spelling.

These boxes will help you with the activity.

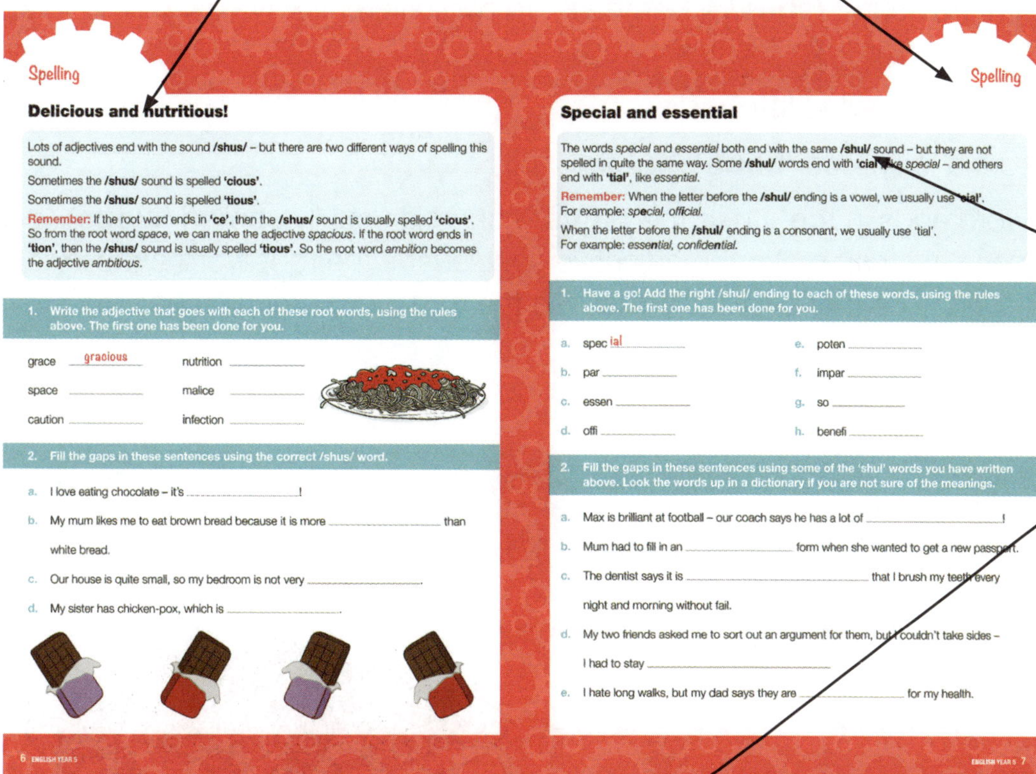

Spelling

Delicious and nutritious!

Lots of adjectives end with the sound **/shus/** – but there are two different ways of spelling this sound.

Sometimes the **/shus/** sound is spelled **'cious'**.

Sometimes the **/shus/** sound is spelled **'tious'**.

Remember: If the root word ends in **'ce'**, then the **/shus/** sound is usually spelled **'cious'**. So from the root word *space*, we can make the adjective *spacious*. If the root word ends in **'tion'**, then the **/shus/** sound is usually spelled **'tious'**. So the root word *ambition* becomes the adjective *ambitious*.

1. Write the adjective that goes with each of these root words, using the rules above. The first one has been done for you.

grace gracious — nutrition ______

space ______ — malice ______

caution ______ — infection ______

2. Fill the gaps in these sentences using the correct /shus/ word.

a. I love eating chocolate – it's ______!

b. My mum likes me to eat brown bread because it is more ______ than white bread.

c. Our house is quite small, so my bedroom is not very ______.

d. My sister has chicken-pox, which is ______.

6 ENGLISH YEAR 5

Spelling

Special and essential

The words *special* and *essential* both end with the same **/shul/** sound – but they are not spelled in quite the same way. Some **/shul/** words end with **'cial'**, like *special* – and others end with **'tial'**, like *essential*.

Remember: When the letter before the **/shul/** ending is a vowel, we usually use **'cial'**. For example: *special, official*.

When the letter before the **/shul/** ending is a consonant, we usually use 'tial'. For example: *essential, confidential*.

1. Have a go! Add the right /shul/ ending to each of these words, using the rules above. The first one has been done for you.

a. spec ial — e. poten ______

b. par ______ — f. impar ______

c. essen ______ — g. so ______

d. offi ______ — h. benefi ______

2. Fill the gaps in these sentences using some of the 'shul' words you have written above. Look the words up in a dictionary if you are not sure of the meanings.

a. Max is brilliant at football – our coach says he has a lot of ______!

b. Mum had to fill in an ______ form when she wanted to get a new passport.

c. The dentist says it is ______ that I brush my teeth every night and morning without fail.

d. My two friends asked me to sort out an argument for them, but I couldn't take sides – I had to stay ______.

e. I hate long walks, but my dad says they are ______ for my health.

ENGLISH YEAR 5 7

This is the instruction text. It tells you what to do.

Follow the instruction to complete the activity.

You might have to write on lines, in boxes, draw or circle things.

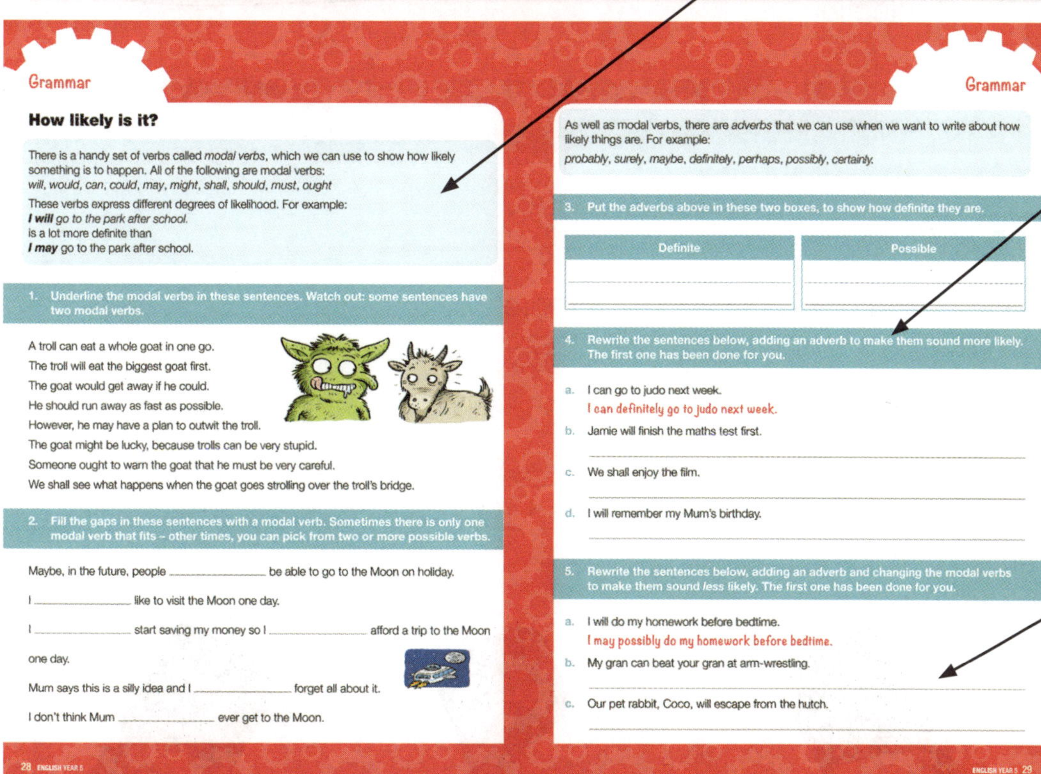

Grammar

How likely is it?

There is a handy set of verbs called *modal verbs*, which we can use to show how likely something is to happen. All of the following are modal verbs:

will, would, can, could, may, might, shall, should, must, ought

These verbs express different degrees of likelihood. For example:

***I will** go to the park after school.*

is a lot more definite than

***I may** go to the park after school.*

1. Underline the modal verbs in these sentences. Watch out: some sentences have two modal verbs.

A troll can eat a whole goat in one go.

The troll will eat the biggest goat first.

The goat would get away if he could.

He should run away as fast as possible.

However, he may have a plan to outwit the troll.

The goat might be lucky, because trolls can be very stupid.

Someone ought to warn the goat that he must be very careful.

We shall see what happens when the goat goes strolling over the troll's bridge.

2. Fill the gaps in these sentences with a modal verb. Sometimes there is only one modal verb that fits – other times, you can pick from two or more possible verbs.

Maybe, in the future, people ______ be able to go to the Moon on holiday.

I ______ like to visit the Moon one day.

I ______ start saving my money so I ______ afford a trip to the Moon one day.

Mum says this is a silly idea and I ______ forget all about it.

I don't think Mum ______ ever get to the Moon.

28 ENGLISH YEAR 5

Grammar

As well as modal verbs, there are *adverbs* that we can use when we want to write about how likely things are. For example:

probably, surely, maybe, definitely, perhaps, possibly, certainly.

3. Put the adverbs above in these two boxes, to show how definite they are.

Definite	Possible

4. Rewrite the sentences below, adding an adverb to make them sound more likely. The first one has been done for you.

a. I can go to judo next week.
I can definitely go to judo next week.

b. Jamie will finish the maths test first.

c. We shall enjoy the film.

d. I will remember my Mum's birthday.

5. Rewrite the sentences below, adding an adverb and changing the modal verbs to make them sound *less* likely. The first one has been done for you.

a. I will do my homework before bedtime.
I may possibly do my homework before bedtime.

b. My gran can beat your gran at arm-wrestling.

c. Our pet rabbit, Coco, will escape from the hutch.

ENGLISH YEAR 5 29

If you need help, ask an adult!

Spelling

Delicious and nutritious!

Lots of adjectives end with the sound **/shus/** – but there are two different ways of spelling this sound.

Sometimes the **/shus/** sound is spelled **'cious'**.

Sometimes the **/shus/** sound is spelled **'tious'**.

Remember: If the root word ends in **'ce'**, then the **/shus/** sound is usually spelled **'cious'**. So from the root word *space*, we can make the adjective *spacious*. If the root word ends in **'tion'**, then the **/shus/** sound is usually spelled **'tious'**. So the root word *ambition* becomes the adjective *ambitious*.

1. Write the adjective that goes with each of these root words, using the rules above. The first one has been done for you.

grace gracious

space ______

caution ______

nutrition ______

malice ______

infection ______

2. Fill the gaps in these sentences using the correct /shus/ word.

a. I love eating chocolate – it's ______!

b. My mum likes me to eat brown bread because it is more ______ than white bread.

c. Our house is quite small, so my bedroom is not very ______.

d. My sister has chicken-pox, which is ______.

Special and essential

The words *special* and *essential* both end with the same **/shul/** sound – but they are not spelled in quite the same way. Some **/shul/** words end with **'cial'**, like *special* – and others end with **'tial'**, like *essential*.

Remember: When the letter before the **/shul/** ending is a vowel, we usually use **'cial'**.
For example: *sp**e**cial, offi**c**ial.*

When the letter before the **/shul/** ending is a consonant, we usually use 'tial'.
For example: *esse**n**tial, confide**n**tial.*

1. Have a go! Add the right /shul/ ending to each of these words, using the rules above. The first one has been done for you.

a. spec ial__________

b. par ____________

c. essen ____________

d. offi ____________

e. poten ____________

f. impar ____________

g. so ____________

h. benefi ____________

2. Fill the gaps in these sentences using some of the 'shul' words you have written above. Look the words up in a dictionary if you are not sure of the meanings.

a. Max is brilliant at football – our coach says he has a lot of ________________!

b. Mum had to fill in an ____________ form when she wanted to get a new passport.

c. The dentist says it is ____________________ that I brush my teeth every night and morning without fail.

d. My two friends asked me to sort out an argument for them, but I couldn't take sides – I had to stay ____________________

e. I hate long walks, but my dad says they are ____________ for my health.

Spelling

Ant machine

Look at this word: *important.* Can you spot the **'ant'** at the end?
The machine below turns root words into new words, ending with **'ant'**, **'ance'**, **'ancy'** or **'ation'**. Some root words will make new words with most or all of these endings.

Remember: Not all root words will give you a real word in each box of the ant machine. Use a dictionary to check your words if you're not sure whether they are real.

1. Have a go! Try putting the root words below into the 'ant' machine. Write the root words in, and see how many new real words you can make. The first one has been done for you.

~~import~~ * observ * hesit * expect * toler * relev * ten * assist

Ent machine

Look at this word: *frequent.* Can you spot the **'ent'** at the end?

The machine below turns root words into new words, ending with **'ent'**, **'ence'**, **'ency'**.

Some root words will make new words with most or all of these endings. Others will only make words with one or two of the endings.

If you put the root word 'frequ' into the 'ent' machine, it makes two new words – *frequent* and *frequency*.

1. Try putting the root words below into the 'ent' machine. Write the root words in, and see how many new real words you can make.

innoc * dec * confid * obedi * independ * evid * differ

Are you able?

Lots of words end in **'able'** or **'ably'**. Look at these examples:

- *considerable – considerably*
- *adorable – adorably*
- *applicable – applicably*

Some words have endings that sound like these, but are spelled **'ible'** or **'ibly'**. For example

- *possible – possibly*
- *visible – visibly*

So how do you decide whether a word ends in **'able'**/**'ably'** or **'ible'**/**'ibly'**? Luckily, there is a rule that helps. If there is a word with the same root, ending in **'ation'**, then we normally use the **'able'**/**'ably'** spelling.

That means that if you are wondering how to spell *considerable*, you can think of the word *consideration* – and that tells you that it must end in **'able'**, not in **'ible'**.

1. Use the 'ation' rule above to help you fill in this chart.

Which spelling is right?	Is there an 'ation' word?	So is it 'able' or 'ible'?	So is it 'ably' or 'ibly'?
sensable or *sensible*	No – sensiblation is not a real word	sensible	sensibly
adorable or *adorible*	Yes – adoration	adorable	adorably
possable or *possible*			
applicable or *applicible*			
incredable or *incredible*			
terrable or *terrible*			
visable or *visible*			

No stress!

When you add a suffix to a root word that ends with **'fer'**, sometimes you have to double the final **'r'**, like this: *refer – referring – referred.*

But sometimes, you don't have to double the **'r'** when you add a suffix to this kind of word. For example: *refer – reference – referee.*

How can you work out whether the **'r'** needs to be doubled or not? Luckily, there is a simple rule. If the **'fer'** syllable is stressed after you add the suffix, then you double the **'r'**. If the **'fer'** syllable *isn't* stressed, then you don't double the **'r'**. (If you say *referring* out loud, you will hear that the **'fer'** syllable is stressed, or said with extra emphasis. If you say *referee* out loud, you will hear that the extra emphasis is on the **'ee'** syllable, not on the **'fer'** syllable.)

1. Complete the table, making sure you follow the rule.

Root	Suffix	New word
prefer	ing	
prefer	ed	
prefer	ence	
transfer	ing	
transfer	ed	
transfer	ence	
defer	ing	
defer	ed	
defer	ence	
infer	ing	
infer	ed	
infer	ence	

Prefixes with hyphens

Normally when we add a prefix to a root word, we stick the prefix on to the front of the word without a hyphen, like this: *re + position = reposition*

However, sometimes we need to put a hyphen between the prefix and the root word. Usually we do this when the prefix ends in a vowel, and the root word begins with the same vowel. For example:
re + enter = re-enter, not *reenter*
co + owner = co-owner, not *coowner*

Adding a hyphen to words like these makes them easier to pronounce and to understand.

Normally, if the prefix ends with a vowel and the root word starts with a different vowel, you don't need to add a hyphen. For example:
pro + active = proactive, not *pro-active*

But some prefixes always have a hyphen after them, whatever the root word is like. For example, you always need a hyphen with these prefixes:
'ex' – *ex-soldier*
'self' – *self-portrait*
'all' – *all-encompassing*

1. Use the rules above to help you fill in this chart.

Prefix	Root word	New word
re	active	reactive
ex	husband	
co	habit	
re	enact	
co	operate	
all	inclusive	
self	respect	
pre	enrolment	
pre	date	

Except after 'c'

Write **'ie'** when it is a long **/ee/** sound, except after **'c'** when you should write **'ei'**.
Examples: *chief*, *field*, *shield*, *ceiling*, *deceive*, *receive.*
Exceptions: *either*, *height*, *leisure*, *neither*, *seize*, *their*, *weird.*

Write **'ei'** when the sound is not a long **/ee/** sound, especially when the sound is long **'a'** (**/ay/**).
Examples: *eight*, *freight*, *height*, *neighbour*, *reign*, *weigh.*
Exceptions: *friend*, *mischief.*

1. Add 'ie' or 'ei' in the gaps below.

ach_____ve	bes_____ge	th_____r
p_____rce	rel_____f	h_____ght
gr_____f	rec_____ve	f_____rce
c_____ling	w_____gh	s_____ze
_____ght	f_____ld	_____ther

Spelling

It's tough!

Some **'ough'** words are pronounced in the same way as each other.

1. Look at the 'ough' words below, and write them in the correct boxes to show how they are pronounced.

plough * though * thought * brought * rough * enough * nought * soup
Slough * although * coupon * cough * ought * trough * tough * thorough
dough * borough * bought * fought * through

'ough' sounds like 'or' as in *fort*

____

____

'ough' sounds like 'oo' as in *moon*

____

'ough' sounds like 'er' as in *manner*

____

'ough' sounds like 'uff' as in *cuff*

____

'ough' sounds like 'ow' as in *now*

____

'ough' sounds like 'off' as in *toffee*

____

'ough' sounds like 'ow' as in *snow*

____

2. Pick three 'ough' words with different pronunciations, and write a sentence using each word.

____

____

____

Shhh...

Some words – like *wrinkle* – have letters which we don't pronounce. These are often called *silent letters*. The silent letters in some words used to be pronounced a long time ago. For example, in the Middle Ages, people pronounced the **'k'** in words like *knight* and *knife*.

1. Read the words below, and circle the silent letters.

knight lamb gnat knife plumber
gnome island solemn psychology whistle
wren thumb hymn doubt bomb
gnash psalm pterodactyl thistle comb
design autumn knee listen bristle

2. Sort the words into the boxes below, to show which words have which silent letters.

silent 'b' ______________________

____

silent 'g' ______________________

____

silent 'k' ______________________

____

silent 'n' ______________________

____

silent 'p' ______________________

____

silent 's' ______________________

____

silent 't' ______________________

____

silent 'w' ______________________

____

Spelling

How much farther, Father?

The words *farther* and *father* are *homophones*: they are spelled differently, and they have different meanings, but they sound the same. *Farther* means *further*. *Father* is another name for *dad*.
Homophones are often used in jokes like the ones you find in Christmas crackers.
Here's an example:

Q When is a bucket unwell?
A When it is a little pail.

1. Solve the clues below with one word, and then match the word to its homophone. The first one is done for you.

Clues	Answers	Homophones
To leave quickly	flee	serial
A male parent	____________	heard
Eat a bowl of this for breakfast	____________	guessed
A visitor	____________	flea
A group of animals	____________	draft
A cold current of air	____________	farther

2. Use the words *father* and *farther* to fill the gaps in the sentences below.

a. Dan's ____________ is a firefighter.

b. It was getting dark as we wandered ____________ and ____________ into the woods.

c. I asked my ____________ how much ____________ we had to go.

d. Did your ____________ never tell you that it's rude to do that?

e. I managed to run 5km, but my ____________ ran even ____________.

Homophone search

1. Write the homophone or near-homophone for each of the words below. The first one has been done for you.

isle aisle

guessed ______

aloud ______

herd ______

led ______

affect ______

bridle ______

mourning ______

father ______

assent ______

dissent ______

2. Now find the words you have written in the grid below. Search across and down. Circle them as you find them.

a	s	c	e	n	t	i	h	o	c	k	s	s	t
i	p	s	d	e	s	c	e	n	t	m	f	l	o
s	i	r	d	a	f	l	a	l	l	o	w	e	d
l	e	e	m	t	a	g	r	t	u	r	n	a	e
e	g	b	e	b	r	i	d	a	l	n	b	d	f
g	u	e	s	t	i	l	o	m	a	i	r	g	f
f	e	a	g	r	o	o	i	d	e	n	i	u	e
f	a	r	t	h	e	r	l	f	m	g	m	e	c
t	r	g	o	l	a	r	p	e	n	a	l	r	t

3. Choose a homophone pair from the homophones on this page. Write two sentences – one using each word in the pair. Your sentences need to show that you understand what the homophones mean, and can spell them correctly.

______

______

Spelling

Crossophone

1. The answers to the crossword clues below are all homophones or near-homophones.

Across

1. A basic belief.
5. Your dad.
6. Go before.
9. To change something is to a ______ it.
10. I would never have g ______ that you were such a good dancer!
12. A word that means the same as *further*.
14. A very heavy metal.
16. A dry and barren place.
17. All the things you need if you're going to do some writing.

Down

1. We p______ the school as we walked into town.
2. When someone says something nice about you, it's a ______.
3. Someone who can see into the future.
4. Bad weather often has an ______ on people's plans.
7. When you go down the mountain, you make a ______.
8. Rain may ______ our plan to have a picnic.
9. A word that means the same as *permitted*.
10. A visitor who comes to stay.
11. The money you might make if you sell something.
13. Have you h______ the latest news?
15. A cold gust of air.

Story language

The story below includes lots of synonyms (words with similar meanings) – but some of them are too informal, and some of them are too boring.

1. Read the story.
2. Highlight or underline the synonyms that you think are most interesting and appropriate for the story.

Prince Charming was a **good-looking** / **handsome** / **brave** / **charming** young **man** / **guy** / **youth** / **prince**. He heard that a **cute** / **beautiful** / **nice** / **pretty** princess was sleeping in an **ancient** / **old** / **impregnable** / **enormous** castle and could only be woken with a kiss. The problem was that the castle was protected by a **huge** / **prickly** / **thorny** / **big** hedge. The hedge was so **prickly** / **dangerous** / **high** / **perilous** that many knights had died trying to climb over it.

It was a **horrible** / **nasty** / **fearsome** / **scary** sight. The thorns were as big as **daggers** / **kitchen knives** / **dragon's teeth** / **rulers**, and **skeletons** / **corpses** / **dead bodies** / **cadavers** hung from them. The air was filled with the **stench** / **pong** / **smell** / **aroma** of their rotting bodies.

But Prince Charming was not **scared** / **deterred** / **put off** / **frightened**. He walked **bravely** / **courageously** / **determinedly** / **quickly** towards the hedge and, to his amazement, the thorns turned to **beautiful** / **lovely** / **nice** / **pretty** flowers. That was because the 100-year spell ended at that moment – even though the prince knew nothing about it.

He walked **happily** / **eagerly** / **quickly** / **excitedly** to the castle where he found everybody **snoozing** / **sleeping** / **dozing** / **resting**. Then he found his way to Sleeping Beauty's tower. He had never seen anyone so **nice** / **sweet** / **cute** / **lovely**. Her skin was as pale as **milk** / **snow** / **paper** / **silk** and her lips were as red as **blood** / **roses** / **paint** / **lipstick**.

He kissed her and she awoke with a **jerk** / **start** / **twitch** / **jump**.

"What time is it?" she said **quietly** / **breathlessly** / **curiously** / **sleepily**.

"It's five and twenty past eight in the morning of March the first, 1492."

"Oh, dear," she **moaned** / **sighed** / **groaned** / **complained**, "that's much too early." And she went back to sleep for another **2** / **10** / **100** / **1,000,000** years!

Vocabulary

Official language

Official forms and documents normally use language in a very precise, formal way. They often use complex sentences, imperative forms of verbs and formal, subject-specific vocabulary.

1. **Read this text, which is an extract from DVLA leaflet D100.**
2. **Underline the complex sentences.**
3. **Draw a wavy line under any sentences that use the imperative (commands).**
4. **Draw a ring round words which are formal or subject-specific.**

Driver and Vehicle Licensing Agency (DVLA)

1. PHOTOCARD DRIVING LICENCES
DVLA now only issues photocard driving licences. This is to improve road safety by eliminating impersonation at driving tests and ensuring the person driving a vehicle is qualified to do so.

You will be issued with:

- a photocard; showing
  - the driver's photograph and signature which is electronically copied from the application form
  - categories of vehicles the driver is entitled to drive
- a paper counterpart document, showing
  - your signature (also electronically copied)
  - details of any endorsements, and in the case of a full licence holder, any provisional driving entitlement held.

Note: You must produce *both* the photocard and counterpart if requested by the police or a court. You should also present both parts when taking a driving test. You may also find that other organisations, such as car hire firms and insurance companies, will ask to see both parts.

Drivers will need to renew their photocard licence every ten years until age 70 to keep the photograph up to date. This will not affect the validity period of the entitlement shown on the licence. DVLA will send a reminder when the photograph is due for renewal. Drivers who are required to renew their licence at shorter intervals, for example, for medical reasons, or because they hold entitlement to drive buses or lorries, will not be required to renew their photograph at each renewal.

A formal letter

If you are writing a letter to someone you don't know – for example, to make a complaint or ask for help – you need to use formal language.
Here is one occasion when a formal letter is appropriate:

Luke Jones bought a computer game, but when he tried to load it, the message 'Insufficient data' appeared on his screen. He followed all the instructions, but it still didn't work. He went back to the shop, but the assistant first ignored him, and then refused to give him an exchange or a refund.

1. Read this letter, which Luke wrote to the shop manager.

To the manager,

I got a game from your shop on Saturday when me and my mum was shopping. When I got it home, I stuck it in my computer, but it wouldn't load. I was unhappy. My mum said to take it back to the shop. I came back to the shop and a different guy was on the till. He told me the game was OK and it must be the way I was loading it. I felt bad as my mum wasn't with me and I didn't know what to say.

When I got home my mum said I should write down my complaint, so I am. Please write back to me.

From
Luke Jones, aged 10

2. Rewrite Luke's letter, using more formal language.

Vocabulary

Literal and figurative language

1. Study this table which explains the terms *literal*, *figurative*, *metaphor* and *simile*.
2. Add your own examples to the table.

Literal	Figurative	
	Simile	Metaphor
Straightforward, factual way of saying something	A comparison using *like* or *as*	A direct comparison saying one thing is another
My feet are cold. Ordinary post is slow. He is tall.	My feet are like ice. Ordinary post is as slow as a snail. He is as tall as a giant.	My feet are ice. Ordinary post is snail mail. He is a giant of a man.
Own examples		

Introducing expanded noun phrases

Expanded noun phrases are a way of adding more information about a noun. Sometimes we use nouns in sentences without a lot of extra detail, for example:

- *My friend came round yesterday.*
  In this sentence, *My friend* is a noun phrase. It takes the noun *friend* and gives us a little bit of extra information – it's not just any old friend, it's *my* friend.

However, sometimes you might want to add more detail than this – and that's when expanded noun phrases come in handy. Here's the same sentence with an expanded noun phrase:

- *My best friend, Tom, came round yesterday.*
  We now know a lot more about the friend – it's my best friend, and his name is Tom.
  You can expand a noun phrase even more than this. Look at this example:
- *My zany, football-loving best friend, Tom, came round yesterday.*

1. The noun phrases are underlined in the sentences below. Write the sentences out again, but this time add some extra description or detail to create expanded noun phrases like the examples above. The first one has been done for you.

a. <u>My brother</u> was crying.

Expanded version: My sulky little brother was crying.

b. <u>The dog</u> was barking.

Expanded version: ______________________________

c. <u>A dragon</u> flew overhead.

Expanded version: ______________________________

d. Tom put on <u>his football boots</u>.

Expanded version: ______________________________

e. I sat on <u>the chair</u>.

Expanded version: ______________________________

f. I like <u>spaghetti</u>.

Expanded version: ______________________________

Vocabulary

Slick descriptions

1. Write a sentence about each of the people shown in the pictures, using expanded noun phrases. The first one has been done for you.

optician

The kind and friendly optician, who liked to put people at their ease, examined the boy's eyes with her instruments.

politician

____

____

musician

____

____

scientist

____

____

magician

____

____

2. Look back at the sentences you have written and circle the expanded noun phrases.

'Verbing' nouns and adjectives

You can turn some nouns and adjectives into verbs by adding the suffixes **'ate'**, **'ise'** and **'ify'**. Sometimes you have to take off another suffix or change the root word a bit first. Here are some examples:

noun: *accommodation*	+ **'ate'**	= verb: *accommodate*
adjective: *active*	+ **'ate'**	= verb: *activate*
adjective: *authentic*	+ **'ate'**	= verb: *authenticate*
noun: *stimulus*	+ **'ate'**	= verb: *stimulate*
noun: *apology*	+ **'ise'**	= verb: *apologise*
noun: *demon*	+ **'ise'**	= verb: *demonise*
noun: *drama*	+ **'ise'**	= verb: *dramatise*
noun: *beauty*	+ **'ify'**	= verb: *beautify*
noun: *electricity*	+ **'ify'**	= verb: *electrify*
noun: *purity*	+ **'ify'**	= verb: *purify*

1. Add suffixes to the words below to make new words. Write a short definition for each new word you make.

reunite + 'ify' = ______________________

solid + 'ify' = ______________________

advert + 'ise' = ______________________

category + 'ise' = ______________________

facility + 'ate' = ______________________

origin + 'ate' = ______________________

____

____

____

____

____

____

____

Vocabulary

Verbs and their opposites

You can change the meaning of some verbs – or even change them into their opposite – by adding a prefix. It's a bit like being a magician: you can make verbs *appear and **dis**appear.* You have to be careful, though – you can't do this with every verb. The main prefixes which can be used to change the meaning of a verb into its opposite are **'dis'**, **'de'** and **'mis'**.

1. Look at the verbs below. Add one of the prefixes above to each verb, to change the meaning. Remember: It needs to make a real word.

connect + dis = disconnect

behave + ________ = ____________________

approve + ________ = ____________________

hear + ________ = ____________________

clutter + ________ = ____________________

understand + ________ = ____________________

like + ________ = ____________________

throne + ________ = ____________________

obey + ________ = ____________________

mystify + ________ = ____________________

2. Add a prefix to the verbs in these sentences so that the sentences change their meaning.

a. The soldiers _____activated the mines that had been buried in the ground.

b. My teacher, Mrs Turner, _____approves of people who give in their homework late.

c. The letter never reached my cousin because I _____addressed the envelope.

d. I _____believed my brother when he said he had seen a pixie in our garden.

e. We _____trusted the enemy when they told us they wanted to surrender.

Using the perfect form of verbs

We use the *perfect form* of verbs when we want to talk or write about something that has already happened in the past. Here's an example of the *present perfect* form:

- *I have eaten all the cake*.

You can tell that this sentence is in the present perfect, because the helping verb *have* is in the present tense, but the main verb *eaten* is in the past tense. The sentence is set in the present, but it tells us about something that has already happened.

Here's an example of the *past perfect* form:

- *Mum **had left** the cake out on the table.*

You can tell that this is in the past perfect, because the helping verb *had* is in the past tense, and so is the main verb *left*. So this sentence is talking about something that had already happened at some point in the past.

1. Write *present perfect* or *past perfect* next to each of the sentences below.

a. I had never seen such an enormous dog. ____________________.

b. Gran has made a delicious chicken pie for tea. ____________________.

c. After I had opened my birthday presents, I gave everyone a thank-you hug. __________.

d. I have always wanted a pet iguana. ____________________.

e. Mum had put the biscuits on a very high shelf. ____________________.

2. Rewrite the sentences below so that they use the past perfect form.

a. I have spent all morning tidying my bedroom.

____

b. Sam looked everywhere for his pen.

____

c. Ellie has gone to the shops to get some sweets.

____

How likely is it?

There is a handy set of verbs called *modal verbs*, which we can use to show how likely something is to happen. All of the following are modal verbs:
will, *would*, *can*, *could*, *may*, *might*, *shall*, *should*, *must*, *ought*

These verbs express different degrees of likelihood. For example:
I will *go to the park after school.*
is a lot more definite than
I may go to the park after school.

1. Underline the modal verbs in these sentences. Watch out: some sentences have two modal verbs.

A troll can eat a whole goat in one go.
The troll will eat the biggest goat first.
The goat would get away if he could.
He should run away as fast as possible.
However, he may have a plan to outwit the troll.
The goat might be lucky, because trolls can be very stupid.
Someone ought to warn the goat that he must be very careful.
We shall see what happens when the goat goes strolling over the troll's bridge.

2. Fill the gaps in these sentences with a modal verb. Sometimes there is only one modal verb that fits – other times, you can pick from two or more possible verbs.

Maybe, in the future, people ________________ be able to go to the Moon on holiday.

I ________________ like to visit the Moon one day.

I ________________ start saving my money so I ________________ afford a trip to the Moon one day.

Mum says this is a silly idea and I ________________ forget all about it.

I don't think Mum ________________ ever get to the Moon.

As well as modal verbs, there are *adverbs* that we can use when we want to write about how likely things are. For example:

probably, *surely*, *maybe*, *definitely*, *perhaps*, *possibly*, *certainly*.

3. Put the adverbs above in these two boxes, to show how definite they are.

Definite	Possible

4. Rewrite the sentences below, adding an adverb to make them sound more likely. The first one has been done for you.

a. I can go to judo next week.

I can definitely go to judo next week.

b. Jamie will finish the maths test first.

c. We shall enjoy the film.

d. I will remember my Mum's birthday.

5. Rewrite the sentences below, adding an adverb and changing the modal verbs to make them sound *less* likely. The first one has been done for you.

a. I will do my homework before bedtime.

I may possibly do my homework before bedtime.

b. My gran can beat your gran at arm-wrestling.

c. Our pet rabbit, Coco, will escape from the hutch.

Grammar

All in a good clause

Relative clauses give more information about nouns. They are usually introduced by a relative pronoun – for example:
who, *which*, *whose*, *where*, *when*, *that.*

1. Choose a relative pronoun from the list above to introduce the relative clauses below. The first one has been done for you.

Noun (in bold)	Relative pronoun	Relative clause
This is the **programme**	that	I told you about.
Cabot is the **explorer**		discovered Newfoundland.
I wish to see the **boy**		football boots were left in the classroom.
Please upgrade the **computers**		are in the computer room.
I enjoyed the **day**		I won the race.
This is for the **girl**		lost her history book.
Here is the **canteen**		we eat lunch.
The telescope is an **instrument**		makes it possible to see distant planets.
I first saw the **girl**		she was playing tennis.
Kari was a new **pupil**		childhood had been spent in Kosovo.
Iceland is a **country**		is north of Scotland.
This is the **street**		my gran lives.

It's all relative

As well as adding more information about a noun, you can also use relative clauses to add more information about another clause. Here's an example:
We took a long time to walk home, which meant we missed tea.
Here, the *which* refers back to the whole of the first clause in the sentence, *We took a long time to walk home.*

1. Draw lines to link the two halves of the sentences below. All of the sentences include a relative pronoun.

Dad suddenly realised he was wearing odd socks,

Janie walked down the street

Greg is the boy

I ate the sandwich

The mouse disappeared into a tiny hole,

My favourite city is Dublin,

Mrs Baxter introduced the girl

I was getting out of the shower at the very moment

This is the famous athlete

I was ill on Wednesday,

which has many beautiful buildings.

which Mum had made for me.

when you knocked at the door.

where the famous actor lived.

which he found very embarrassing.

whose shoes got lost.

which meant I missed the play.

who won the marathon.

which annoyed the cat.

who was coming to join our class.

Grammar

Making links

There are lots of words that we can use to help us make links within and between sentences and paragraphs.
For example, we can use *adverbs* and *adverbials* like these:
then, *after*, *that*, *this*, *firstly*, *later*, *nearby*, *unfortunately*, *just then.*
We can also use *conjunctions* like these:
although, *and*, *as*, *because*, *but*, *for*, *until*, *when*, *where*, *while.*
Words like these help us to link different ideas in our writing. For example, look at these sentences:
Firstly*, I added four tablespoons of salt to the water.* ***Then*** *I stirred it* ***until*** *the salt dissolved* **and** *the liquid was clear. Five minutes* ***later*** *I heated the liquid to boiling point.*
The words in bold help to show the order in which the actions were done, and how the actions connect to each other. Making links like this is sometimes described as ***building cohesion***. The underlined words all help to make *cohesive links* within and between the sentences.

1. Underline the words and phrases that help to build cohesion in the paragraphs below.

Because I was very hungry, I decided to make myself a sandwich. Firstly, I took two slices of bread, and then I went to the fridge because I wanted to get some cheese. However, there was no cheese in the fridge, so I had to use peanut butter instead.

When I had finally found the peanut butter, I spread it thickly on one of the slices of bread. Then I put the other slice of bread on top. Next, I cut the sandwich into four triangles. I always cut my sandwiches like this. When I had put the sandwich on my favourite plate, I sat down at the table to eat it.

Unfortunately, just at that moment, my sister came running into the room. “Great!” she said. “You’ve made me a sandwich!”

Before I could say a word, she grabbed my sandwich and started to eat it. I tried to stop her, but it was too late. She wolfed that sandwich down, and then asked for more.

2. Read the information text below. Lots of the words and phrases that help to create cohesion have been left out. Write them back in again. Sometimes there is more than one word or phrase you could use – you can choose which you think sounds best. Look back at page 32 if you need a reminder about words and phrases that create cohesion.

The platypus is a most unusual kind of mammal. ______________ other mammals give birth to live young, the female platypus lays two soft-shelled eggs ______________ she incubates for one to two weeks. ______________ the eggs hatch, she feeds the young with milk from her milk glands. The young do not suck on the milk glands. Instead, they ______________ push at the glands and ______________ suck the milk which oozes out into their mother's fur.

Another interesting feature of the platypus is its large, soft beak or bill. It ______________ is so sensitive it is able to detect the small creatures in the water ______________ the platypus feeds upon. Its sensitive beak is invaluable, ______________ the platypus is blind ______________ deaf when it is in the water.

The platypus has a furry body, ______________ four legs with webbed feet. It uses its front legs to paddle ______________ its hind legs to swim, enabling it to swim strongly under the water. Male platypuses have a poison gland on their ankles ______________ they use to fend off enemies. Adult platypuses weigh up to 2.4kg, ______________ males grow up to 60cm ______________ females are slightly smaller. Platypuses are found only in parts of Australia and Tasmania.

Zoos

A class of children have brainstormed about the need for zoos.

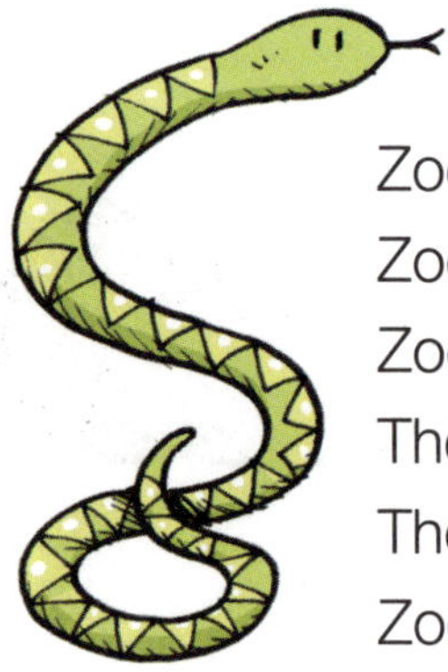

Zoos have saved many animals from extinction.
Zoos are unfair to animals.
Zoos allow people to see animals they would never see otherwise.
The animals change in captivity – sometimes they become neurotic.
They confine animals in small spaces.
Zoos don't give the animals a natural life.
It means people can observe them and learn about them.
The animals have a safer life in the zoo than in the wild.
They provide entertainment for people.
Zoos cost too much and people can't afford to go to them.
It means more people are interested in the animals.
People can see these animals living in the wild on the television; they don't need to go to a zoo.

1. Sort their arguments into two columns, under the headings *For* and *Against*.

For: ______________________

Against: ______________________

2. **Use the arguments you listed on page 34 to help you write two paragraphs in favour of zoos, and two paragraphs against zoos. Don't forget to use words and phrases to build cohesion within and between your paragraphs – look back at page 32 if you need a reminder about this.**

In favour of zoos ______________________________

____

____

____

____

____

____

____

Against zoos: ______________________________

____

____

____

____

____

____

____

Crystal clear commas

There are lots of reasons why commas are useful. Here are a couple of reasons that you probably already know:

- They help to separate items in a list.
- They can help to make a longer or more complex sentence, like this one, easier to read.

Commas can also help to make information clearer. For example, these two sentences mean different things, but the only difference between them is the commas:
All the children who handed in their homework late are in trouble with Mr Marsh.
All the children, who handed in their homework late, are in trouble with Mr Marsh.

The first sentence means that Mr Marsh is cross with those children who handed in their homework late – there might be other children with whom Mr Marsh is not cross.
The second sentence means that Mr Marsh is cross with **all** the children, and they **all** handed in their homework late. The commas are needed to make this clear!

1. Add commas to make the meanings of these sentences clearer.

a. The dogs who had rolled about in the mud were given baths.
(Add commas so that you can tell that all the dogs were given baths.)

b. Grandmas who like playing with their grandchildren have lots of fun.
(Add commas so that you can tell the sentence is about all grandmas.)

c. The boys who broke the window were told off.
(Add commas so that the sentence is about all the boys.)

d. The flowers which were my mum's pride and joy got squashed.
(Add commas so that you can tell that all the flowers got squashed.)

2. Add or cross out commas in these sentences so that the meaning changes.

a. I finished my cake sadly.

b. Let's eat, James!

c. Don't, stop!

d. As I was eating the table collapsed.

e. While Mum was cooking the baby started crying.

3. Rewrite these sentences, adding the missing commas. Look back at page 36 for some examples to help you

a. The soldiers who had been injured in battle were taken to the hospital.

____

b. Trombones which make a very loud noise have been banned from the school orchestra.

____

c. The runners who were on the uphill stretch of the race were puffed out.

____

d. My favourite breakfast which consists of cornflakes toast orange juice and porridge was waiting for me when I came downstairs.

____

____

e. The teachers who are often annoyed with me were waiting for me to come in after lunch.

____

f. On my birthday which comes just before Christmas I received a new computer game a pair of headphones a book and two pairs of socks as presents.

____

____

g. The sharks which had injured fins swam slowly round and round.

____

h. Outside the shops which are currently closed for refurbishment I met Jamie Alisha and Ben.

____

Punctuating Rapunzel

Commas are used like brackets to mark off extra information inserted into a sentence. For example:

- sentence: *Rapunzel lived in a tower.*
- sentence + extra information: *Rapunzel, a girl with very long hair, lived in a tower.*

1. Read these sentences. For each one, find the additional information and place a comma before and after it.

The tower a tall building without any steps was Rapunzel's home.

An old woman to whom the tower belonged kept her prisoner.

She would shout her voice croaking cruelly "Rapunzel, let down your hair!"

Rapunzel's hair like a long ladder hung down from the window.

The old woman who was more agile than she looked scrambled up Rapunzel's hair.

A handsome prince who was hiding nearby saw everything that happened.

2. Write three more sentences about Rapunzel, each with correctly punctuated additional information.

Perfect parentheses

A *parenthesis* is a word or phrase which has been added to a sentence, a bit like an afterthought. One way of telling whether a word or phrase is a parenthesis is to try taking it out of the sentence. If the rest of the sentence still makes sense, then you know that the words you removed are a parenthesis.

Here are some sentences where the parenthesis has been underlined. If you read the sentence without the parenthesis, it still makes sense.
The elephants, which had been working all day, were getting tired and hungry.
My friend Cara (who lives next door) has red hair.
The pirates – beards bristling and eyes flashing – boarded the unsuspecting merchant ship.

As you can see from these examples, parentheses normally have punctuation before and after them, to mark them out from the rest of the sentence. There are three different types of punctuation you can use with parentheses: commas, brackets and dashes.

- We use **commas** when the idea in the parenthesis is really an important part of the sentence – it's not a separate idea, it just adds extra information to the sentence.
- We use **brackets** when the idea in the parenthesis isn't really essential to the meaning of the sentence – it's quite useful or interesting, but you could easily leave it out.
- We use **dashes** when we really want to draw attention to the parenthesis. We normally only use dashes when the idea in the parenthesis is unusual, funny or startling in some way.

1. Add the best sort of punctuation to use around the parentheses in these sentences.

a. The ducks swimming serenely on the pond were suddenly disturbed by a loud noise.

b. My uncle Sam whose middle name is Albert loves karaoke.

c. The Second World War which took place between 1939 and 1945 was a time of great hardship for many people.

d. I was sitting quietly in the kitchen when suddenly crash bang wallop I heard a terrible noise from overhead.

e. I love Saturdays which always seem to take forever to come because that is the day when I go to see Gran and Grandpa.

f. Suddenly the door was flung open knocking my little sister flying and a huge giant shouldered his way into the room.

Twisted lists

This punctuation mark **:** is called a *colon*. One of the main ways we use colons is to introduce a list. Here are a couple of examples:

I got some unusual presents for my birthday: a flying alien, a pet lizard and a bag of toffees.
Four of my best friends came to help me try out the flying alien: Ashley, Meena, Zac and Jake.

Watch out, though – you don't always need a colon before a list. You only use a colon when the clause before it makes complete sense on its own. *I got some unusual presents for my birthday* makes sense on its own, so we use a colon.
We wouldn't use a colon to introduce this list:
At my birthday party we ate pizza, crisps, grapes and cake.
That's because *At my birthday party we ate* doesn't make sense on its own.

1. Add punctuation to these lists. Some of them need colons, but not all of them. They all need commas and full stops.

a. The wizard threw a lot of disgusting things into the cauldron snakes' tongues grasshoppers' legs mud and rotten tomatoes

b. My favourite hobbies are football street dance trampolining and sleeping

c. There are a lot of children in my family four brothers two sisters and fourteen cousins

d. There was a long queue ahead of us at the vet's three cats two dogs a rabbit and four guinea pigs

2. Turn these clauses into lists starting with colons. You can make up what goes in each list. The first one has been done for you.

a. I used all these things to make a model robot: an old cereal box, a roller skate, an egg box and my mum's sunglasses.

b. There are lots of places in the world that I would like to visit ____________________

____

c. Under my bed I found some unexpected things ____________________

d. I made a delicious drink out of all my favourite fruits ____________________

Helpful hyphens

We use *hyphens* when we want to join two words (or parts of words) together.
One of the main reasons for using a hyphen is to avoid ambiguity. There is a big difference between the meanings of these two phrases, even though they use exactly the same words:

- *a man-eating lion*
- *a man eating lion*

The first one is a dangerous wild beast. The second one is a man with a strange taste in food! So, if you want to make sure that your meaning is clear and not ambiguous, you sometimes need to use a hyphen.

1. Add the missing hyphen to each sentence to make the meaning clear.

a. Around 100 odd people went to the school concert.
b. Jamie's dad is a used car salesman.
c. Al Capone was a well known gangster.
d. In winter I like to wear a fleece lined coat.
e. The top earning film this year was *Delilah Duck's Day Out.*
f. The band One Convention released this year's best selling album.
g. I found a half eaten chocolate bar at the bottom of my bag.

2. Explain the difference between these pairs of phrases. The first one has been done for you.

best selling toy and *best-selling toy:* 'Best selling toy' could mean the best toy that does some selling. 'Best-selling toy' means the toy that sells the best.

second hand clothing and *second-hand clothing:* ______________________

____

two month old kittens and *two-month-old kittens:* ______________________

____

a half cooked meal and *a half-cooked meal:* ______________________

____

Bullet points

Bullet points are very useful when you want to make sure that important information stands out clearly. The way to punctuate bullet points depends on how they are worded.

Some bullet points consist of a whole grammatical sentence, like these.
Here are some of the activities we will do at my party:

- *We will throw wet sponges at my dad.*
- *We will eat pizza.*
- *We will climb on the climbing wall.*

You can see that these bullet points are all punctuated like proper sentences, with capital letters and full stops.
Sometimes, bullet points do not consist of a whole grammatical sentence.
At my party we will:

- *throw wet sponges at my dad*
- *eat pizza*
- *climb on the climbing wall.*

It's a good idea to put a full stop at the end of the last bullet point, to show it's the end of the list. Some people like to use a comma (or even a semicolon) at the end of each bullet point in this kind of list, but that is not essential.
The main rule when punctuating bullet points is – be consistent. Make sure the whole list is punctuated in the same way.

1. Add punctuation and capital letters where necessary to the following bullet point lists.

here are some rules for looking after your pet rabbits

- give them space to hop about freely
- make sure they have plenty of fresh water
- offer them lots of green, leafy vegetables

equipment you might need for your rabbits includes

- bowls for food and water
- a hutch
- a brush, if your rabbits have long fur

Room For One More

Read the passage from the story. Then answer these questions.

How difficult it was to sleep in that strange bed! She wrestled with the duvet and thumped the pillow; she turned her back on the flimsy curtains; she wished she had never come up to London.

At midnight she heard the grandfather clock whirr and strike; and then she heard the gravel in the driveway crunch. At once she jumped out of bed and crossed the room and just peeped between the curtains.

What she could see was a gleaming black hearse. But there was no coffin in it, and no flowers. No, the hearse was packed out with living people: a crush of talking, laughing, living people.

Then the driver of the hearse looked straight up at her, as she peeped between the curtains.

"There's room for one more." That's what he said. She could hear his voice quite clearly. Then she tugged the curtains so they crossed over, and ran back across the room, and jumped into bed, and pulled the duvet up over her head. And when she woke up the next morning, she really wasn't sure whether it was all a dream or not.

That day, she went shopping. In the big store, she did Levis Jeanswear on the fifth floor; she did Adidas Sportswear and that was on the sixth floor; and then she did cosmetics and that was on the seventh floor. Carrying two bags in each hand, she walked over to the lift. But when the bell pinged and the doors opened, she saw the lift was already jammed full with people.

The lift attendant looked straight at her as she stood there with her bags. "There's room for one more," he said. And his face was the face of the driver of the hearse.

"No," she said quickly. "No, I'll walk down."

Then the lift door closed with a clang. At once there was a kind of grating screech, and a terrible rattling, then a huge double thud.

The lift in the big store dropped from top to bottom of the shaft, and every single person in it was killed.

Kevin Crossley-Holland

Comprehension

1. At what time did the clock strike? ______________________________

2. What was in the back of the hearse? ______________________________

3. On what floor did the main character end her shopping? ______________________________

4. Why did the lift attendant look familiar to her? ______________________________

5. Which departments in the shop did she visit? ______________________________

   ____

6. How was the main character sleeping? Support your answer with evidence from the text.

   ____

7. *She heard the gravel in the driveway crunch.* Why does the author tell us that the gravel crunches?

   ____

8. *She tugged the curtains so they crossed over, and ran back across the room, and jumped into bed, and pulled the duvet up over her head.* Why has the author used so many commas in this sentence?

   ____

9. Find and copy two statements where the author attempts to build suspense or a sense of fear.

   ____

   ____

10. What is your opinion of this as a scary story? Support your opinion with evidence from the text.

    ____

    ____

Children at work

Read the passage, then answer the questions.

Coal mines were vital for Britain's survival in Victorian times, because people used coal as a source of power, both for heating their homes and for running machines such as steam engines and factory equipment.

In coal mines there were three main jobs open to children: trapper, hurrier and pusher. In early Victorian times, children were hired to work down in the mine from the age of six. On average they worked from five in the morning until approximately five in the afternoon. Their only day off was Sunday, and they earned the equivalent of about ten pence a week for their work.

Children who worked as trappers in mines were required to sit in the dark all day, waiting until they heard the sound of a mine cart coming. Then they opened the door to let the cart through. Trappers were mostly small children, because the doors and passages inside the mine were only 26 inches (about 66 centimetres) high.

Children also worked as hurriers. The hurriers had to help load the mine carts with coal. Once a mine cart was loaded, the hurrier would put on a huge leather belt which had a chain attached to it. Once the belt was secure, the hurrier would get down on his hands and knees and pull the cart along, using the chain. This process could be repeated up to sixteen times a day.

Occasionally, hurriers would have a pusher to help with the cart. Pushers used their heads to push the cart when a hurrier was not strong enough to pull the cart independently. The pusher would be positioned at the rear of the cart.

Working in a mine was not only exhausting and difficult; it was highly dangerous as well. Many miners – children as well as adults – died in accidents. Spending so much time in cramped and unhealthy conditions meant that miners' health suffered. People became increasingly shocked by the conditions that children aged were working in underground. In 1842 a law was passed to prevent women and children aged under 10 from working in mines. By 1900, no boys under 13 were allowed to be miners.

Based on a text by Stephen Moore

Comprehension

1. Why were coal mines so important in Victorian times?

2. How many hours per day did children have to work in coal mines, during early Victorian times?

3. Why might a child who worked in a coal mine look forward to Sunday?

4. Why did hurriers have big leather belts?

5. Why might a tall child or an adult have found it difficult to be a trapper?

6. If you were a Victorian child working in a coal mine, which of the three jobs mentioned in the text would you *least* like to have, and why?

7. Name *two* ways in which working in a coal mine could be dangerous.

8. Why do you think the government eventually decided to pass a law to stop young children being employed in coal mines?

Race against time

Read the passage from the playscript. Then answer the questions.

The scene is a suburban street corner on a sunny Saturday afternoon. Cameron is waiting for someone. He looks anxious.

Cameron: *(to himself)* Where is he? Where is he? He said he'd be here by now. What if he doesn't turn up? No – don't even think about that! He must get here soon – he must!

(Mrs Turner, Cameron's class teacher, comes along. She spots Cameron and stops.)

Mrs Turner: *(concerned)* Cameron? Is everything all right?

Cameron: What? Oh, er ... hi, Mrs Turner. I'm fine. Everything's fine. Honest.

Mrs Turner: Oh well, if you're sure, Cameron. I'll leave you to it. *(She walks on.)*

(Jamie comes running round the corner in a huge rush. He almost knocks Cameron over.)

Jamie: Cameron, mate! Sorry – I didn't see you there. Are you OK?

Cameron: I am now! What took you so long? I've been going mad thinking you weren't coming after all!

Jamie: Hey! Would I let you down? Anyway, we'd better run if we want to get to the park before the others get there.

(The boys start running towards the park.)

Cameron: *(panting)* But what if the others are there already? Or if they've already found the stuff and gone home?

Jamie: You worry too much! Leave it to me, Cam. It'll be fine, you'll see.

(They get to the park.)

Cameron: Come on – we'd better get to the hollow tree fast. I can see Ben and Jamal heading that way. We've got to get there before them!

Jamie: Don't worry – we'll get there easily! Ben and Jamal are really slow runners. And anyway, they don't know exactly where the stuff is hidden. Even if they do get there first, I bet I can put them off the scent.

Cameron: OK ... if you say so. How about you distract them, while I get the stuff out of the hollow tree?

Jamie: Sounds like a good plan. Come on – quick!

Comprehension

1. What is the setting at the start of the playscript?

2. What is the setting at the end?

3. Why is Cameron anxious at the start of the playscript?

4. How do you think Cameron feels when Mrs Turner stops to talk to him? Quote evidence from the text to explain how you know.

5. What kind of person is Jamie? How do you know?

6. Think of three words to describe Cameron, based on what we know about him from the playscript.

7. Why do Jamie and Cameron have to run to the park?

8. Who else is trying to get to the hollow tree?

9. What do you think might be hidden in the hollow tree?

10. Write the conversation between Jamie, Ben and Jamal when Jamie tries to distract the others so that Cameron can get the stuff out of the hollow tree.

My Dad, Your Dad

Read the poem, then answer the questions.

My dad's fatter than your dad,
Yes, my dad's fatter than yours:
If he eats any more he won't fit in the house,
He'll have to live out of doors.

Yes, but my dad's balder than your dad,
Yes, my dad's balder, O.K.,
He's only got two hairs left on his head
And both are turning grey.

Ah, but my dad's thicker than your dad,
My dad's thicker, alright.
He has to look at his watch to see
If it's noon or the middle of the night.

Yes, but my dad's more boring than your dad.
If he ever starts counting sheep
When he can't get to sleep at night, he finds
It's the sheep that go to sleep.

But my dad doesn't mind your dad.
Mine quite likes yours too.
I suppose *they* don't always think much of US!
That's true, I suppose, that's true.

Kit Wright

Comprehension

1. Why do you think the writer chose to use italic text (*like this*) for some verses, and normal text for other verses?

2. What evidence does one of the narrators give for his dad being the thickest?

3. Which of the following is true about the rhyme scheme of the poem?
   a. Lines 2 and 4 rhyme in each verse. ☐
   b. Lines 1 and 3 rhyme in each verse. ☐
   c. Line 1 always rhymes with line 2, and line 3 always rhymes with line 4. ☐

4. Underline the description that best fits the poem.
   sad and thoughtful　　funny and cheeky　　detailed and descriptive

5. What evidence does one of the narrators give for his dad being the most boring?

6. In what ways is the last verse different from all the other verses in the poem?

7. Which verse do you think is the funniest? Give your reasons.

8. Write a short conversation between the two dads, about their children. What might they say? It doesn't have to rhyme.

Choosing your words carefully

When you are writing a piece of text, there are a few things you always need to bear in mind.

- Who do you want to read the text? (***audience***)
- What message do you want them to get from the text? (***purpose***)
- What are texts like this normally like? (***text features***)

Thinking about these things in advance will really help you to choose the right vocabulary for your piece of writing – and it can even help you choose the right grammar and structure, too.

1. Look at the short pieces of text in the table. For each one, say who you think the *audience* is, what the *purpose* is, and what the *key features* of the text are.

Text	Audience	Purpose	Features
Come to beautiful Balton! Enjoy the glorious sunshine on our secluded beach! Why wait to begin your dream holiday?	People who might be interested in buying a holiday.	To persuade people to buy a holiday.	Imperative language (*Come!*), exaggerated language (*glorious, secluded*), rhetorical question (*Why wait ...?*).
Mr Twinkletoes was a tiny elf. He lived all alone at the bottom of Martha's garden. Martha's mummy didn't know he existed, but Martha and the elf were best friends.			
Hedgehogs and porcupines share some important characteristics. For example, they both have spines, or quills.			

Composition

Write a leaflet

The Healthy Schools Initiative is writing a leaflet about how primary schools can encourage a healthy lifestyle. The organisation has already created pages on physical education (PE), after-school activities and healthier menus for school meals. The Healthy Schools Initiative would like you to plan and write the page dedicated to encouraging children aged 7 to 11 to eat fruit at morning break time, rather than less healthy alternatives.

1. Fill in the spider diagram to help you plan your page. Use words and short phrases, not whole sentences. Remember to think about the *audience*, *purpose* and *text features*.

Reasons why eating fruit is good for you:

____

____

____

____

____

____

Reasons why children might enjoy eating fruit:

____

____

____

Title for the page:

____

____

Text features of persuasive leaflets that I will use:

____

____

____

____

What do I want the reader to do after reading the page?

____

____

____

____

2. Use the writing frame below to write a draft of your leaflet page.

heading

picture

Tell the reader why eating fruit is a) good for them and b) fun.

You could use a bullet point list.

Don't forget persuasive language.

You could use bold text or capitals.

Composition

Conveying atmosphere

Authors convey atmosphere in lots of different ways. Sometimes, the way they describe how their story setting ***looks*** helps to convey atmosphere.

Authors can also use the other senses to help the reader enter into the atmosphere of their writing. In the poem below, the nineteenth-century poet John Clare uses ***sounds*** to convey atmosphere.

1. Underline the words and phrases in the poem that you think convey atmosphere best.

Pleasant Sounds

The rustling of leaves under the feet in woods
    and under hedges;
The crumping of cat-ice and snow down wood-rides,
    narrow lanes, and every street causeway;
Rustling through a wood or rather rushing, while the
    wind halloos in the oak-top like thunder;
The rustle of birds' wings startled from their nests or
    flying unseen into the bushes;
The whizzing of larger birds overhead in a wood,
    such as crows, puddocks, buzzards;
The trample of robins and woodlarks on the brown
    leaves, and the patter of squirrels on the green moss;
The fall of an acorn on the ground, the pattering of
    nuts on the hazel branches as they fall from ripeness;
The flirt of the groundlark's wing from the stubbles –
    how sweet such pictures on dewy mornings,
    when the dew flashes from its brown feathers!

2. Make a list of the sounds that *you* often hear at a particular time of day – for example, in the early morning, or at lunchtime at school, or at bedtime...

3. Take some of the ideas you have written above, and use them to write an atmospheric paragraph about the time of day you chose. You can add other details to convey atmosphere as well as sounds. For example, what can you see, smell, taste, touch...?

Using dialogue to keep the plot moving

Writers use *dialogue* in stories for lots of different reasons. Here are just a few:

a. to help the reader imagine the characters and understand what they are like

b. to add variety and keep the reader interested

c. to provide clues about the characters' thoughts, feelings and reasons for doing things

d. to help keep the plot moving.

1. Look at the pieces of *dialogue* below and decide which of the reasons above fits each example best. Write a., b., c. or d. by each example. You can write more than one letter if more than one reason fits.

a. "I'm not sure," said Michael. "I don't think that's a good idea. What if Mum gets really upset?" ____________

b. "I've been saving my pocket money," said Donna, "and now I've got nearly enough to buy…" ____________

c. "Listen, Marta," said Kwezi. "We've got to escape – and I've got a plan. Meet me by the back door at three o'clock – and bring some rope." ____________

2. Imagine you are writing a story about two children who decide to do something extraordinary – it can be anything you like. Write a short conversation between them, where one of the children explains to the other what they are going to do. The dialogue should show the reader what is going to happen next, and help keep the plot moving.

____

____

____

____

____

Now you are going to create dialogue for some new characters: Molly and George.

The story so far…

Molly and George are in dispute over George's paper aeroplane. Molly has objected to George expecting her to fetch and carry for him. Their disagreement seems to be resolved until Molly's turn at throwing the plane ends up with it landing – smack – in George's face.

3. Write the last things Molly and George said to each other.

"____

______________________," said Molly, throwing the plane.

"____

______________________," said George, rubbing his nose.

4. A new character enters the scene. Decide who the new character is and what each character will say to introduce him or her into the story. Remember to use the correct punctuation.

____

____

____

5. Fill in the chart below to show what Molly and George each thought about the new character based on what they said above.

Molly	George

Linking paragraphs

Read the timeline below. You are going to use it to write a short biography of Albert Einstein.

The life of Albert Einstein: a timeline

1879: Albert Einstein is born to Hermann and Pauline Einstein in Ulm, a town near Munich, Germany.

1894: The Einsteins to Pavia, Italy. Albert stays to finish school in Munich. He only lasts a month without his family and then joins them in Italy.

1895: Albert sits a university entrance exam but fails on the arts section. His family send him to the Swiss town of Aarau to finish high school.

1896: Albert graduates high school and enrols in a polytechnic in Zurich.

1898: Albert meets fellow student Mileva Maric and falls in love.

1900: Albert graduates from the polytechnic.

1901: Albert becomes a Swiss citizen.

1902: Hermann Einstein becomes ill and dies.

1903: Albert and Mileva marry.

1904: Albert and Mileva have a son called Hans Albert.

1905: Albert Einstein publishes an article entitled 'On the electrodynamics of moving bodies' in a leading German physics journal. He applies his theory to mass and energy and formulates the famous equation $e=mc^2$.

1910: The Einsteins have a second son, Eduard.

1911: Albert and his family move to Prague where Albert is given a professorship at the university there.

1912: The family then moves to Zurich where Albert is again made a professor.

1914: Einstein become director of the Kaiser Wilhelm institute in Berlin. He and Mileva begin divorce proceedings.

1915: The general theory of relativity is finished.

1919: Albert remarries – his second wife is called Elsa. A solar eclipse proves that Einstein's theory of relativity works.

1921: Albert Einstein is awarded the Nobel Prize for physics.

1. **Read the paragraph below, and then continue the biography from 1895 onwards, using information from the timeline. Don't forget to write in clear paragraphs, using words and phrases such as *then*, *after that*, *this*, *firstly*, *later* to help the reader understand how the ideas in your paragraphs are linked.**

Albert Einstein was born in 1879 in Ulm, Germany. He was the son of Hermann and Pauline Einstein. The Einstein family moved to Pavia, Italy, in 1894 – leaving the 15-year-old Albert in Munich to finish school. However, he lasted only a month before joining his family in Italy.

At the age of 16, Albert sat a university entrance exam. ______________________

Progress chart

Making progress? Tick (✔) the cogs as you complete each section of the book.

	Most questions completed	All questions completed
Spelling		
More practice?		
Vocabulary		
More practice?		
Grammar		
More practice?		
Punctuation		
More practice?		
Comprehension		
More practice?		
Composition		
More practice?		

Answers

The answers are given below. They are referenced by page number and where applicable, question number. The answers usually only include the information the children are expected to give.
Note that answers in literacy will be varied and subjective from child to child, and a fair degree of marker discretion and interpretation is needed, particularly if children's understanding and skills have to be deduced from their answers.

<table>
<tr><th>Page number</th><th>Question number</th><th>Answers</th></tr>
<tr><td>6</td><td>1</td><td>gracious, nutritious, spacious, malicious, cautious, infectious</td></tr>
<tr><td></td><td>2a</td><td>delicious</td></tr>
<tr><td></td><td>2b</td><td>nutritious</td></tr>
<tr><td></td><td>2c</td><td>spacious</td></tr>
<tr><td></td><td>2d</td><td>infectious</td></tr>
<tr><td>7</td><td>1</td><td>special, partial, essential, official, potential, impartial, social, beneficial</td></tr>
<tr><td></td><td>2a</td><td>potential</td></tr>
<tr><td></td><td>2b</td><td>official</td></tr>
<tr><td></td><td>2c</td><td>essential</td></tr>
<tr><td></td><td>2d</td><td>impartial</td></tr>
<tr><td></td><td>2e</td><td>beneficial</td></tr>
<tr><td>8</td><td>1</td><td>'ant': important, observant, hesitant, expectant, tolerant, relevant, tenant, assistant
'ance': importance, observance, hesitance, expectance, tolerance, relevance, assistance
'ancy': hesitancy, expectancy, relevancy, tenancy
'ation': observation, hesitation, expectation, toleration</td></tr>
<tr><td>9</td><td>1</td><td>'ent': innocent, decent, confident, obedient, independent, evident, different
'ence': innocence, confidence, obedience, indepen lence, evidence, difference
'ency': decency, independency</td></tr>
<tr><td>10</td><td>1</td><td>
<table>
<tr><th>Which spelling is right?</th><th>Is there an 'ation' word?</th><th>So is it 'able' or 'ible'?</th><th>So is it 'ably' or 'ibly'?</th></tr>
<tr><td>sensable or sensible</td><td>No – sensiblation is not a real word</td><td>sensible</td><td>sensibly</td></tr>
<tr><td>adorable or adorible</td><td>Yes – adoration</td><td>adorable</td><td>adorably</td></tr>
<tr><td>possable or possible</td><td>No 'ation' word</td><td>possible</td><td>possibly</td></tr>
<tr><td>applicable or applicible</td><td>Yes 'ation' word</td><td>applicable</td><td>applicably</td></tr>
<tr><td>incredable or incredible</td><td>No 'ation' word</td><td>incredible</td><td>incredibly</td></tr>
<tr><td>terrable or terrible</td><td>No 'ation' word</td><td>terrible</td><td>terribly</td></tr>
<tr><td>visable or visible</td><td>No 'ation' word</td><td>visible</td><td>visibly</td></tr>
</table>
</td></tr>
<tr><td>11</td><td>1</td><td>preferring, preferred, preference, transferring, transferred, transference, deferring, deferred, deference, inferring, inferred, inference</td></tr>
<tr><td>12</td><td>1</td><td>reactive, ex-husband, cohabit, re-enter, co-operate, all-inclusive, self-respect, pre-enrolment, predate</td></tr>
<tr><td>13</td><td>1</td><td>achieve, besiege, their, pierce, relief, height, grief, receive, fierce, ceiling, weigh, seize, eight, field, either</td></tr>
<tr><td>14</td><td>1</td><td>Sounds like 'or': brought, thought, nought, ought, bought, fought
Sounds like 'oo': soup, coupon, through
Sounds like 'uff': rough, tough, enough
Sounds like 'er': thorough, borough
Sounds like 'off': cough, trough
Sounds like 'ow' (now): plough, Slough
Sounds like 'ow' (snow): though, although, dough</td></tr>
<tr><td></td><td>2</td><td>Children's own answers.</td></tr>
</table>

<table>
<tr><th>Page number</th><th>Question number</th><th>Answers</th></tr>
<tr><td>15</td><td>1</td><td>knight, lamb, gnat, knife, plumber, gnome, island, solemn, psychology, whistle, wren, thumb, hymn, doubt, bomb, gnash, psalm, pterodactyl, thistle, comb, design, autumn, knee, listen, bristle</td></tr>
<tr><td></td><td>2</td><td>Silent b: lamb, plumber, thumb, doubt, bomb, comb
Silent g: knight, gnat, gnome, gnash, design
Silent k: knight, knife, knee
Silent n: solemn, hymn, autumn
Silent p: psychology, psalm, pterodactyl
Silent s: island
Silent t: whistle, thistle, listen, bristle
Silent w: wren</td></tr>
<tr><td>16</td><td>1</td><td>flee – flea, father – farther, cereal – serial, guest – guessed, herd – heard, draught – draft</td></tr>
<tr><td></td><td>2a</td><td>father</td></tr>
<tr><td></td><td>2b</td><td>farther, farther</td></tr>
<tr><td></td><td>2c</td><td>father, farther</td></tr>
<tr><td></td><td>2d</td><td>father</td></tr>
<tr><td></td><td>2e</td><td>father, farther</td></tr>
<tr><td>17</td><td>1</td><td>isle – aisle, guessed – guest, aloud – allowed, herd – heard, led – lead, affect – effect, bridle – bridal, mourning – morning, father – farther, assent – ascent, dissent – descent</td></tr>
<tr><td></td><td>2</td><td>
<table>
<tr><td>a</td><td>s</td><td>c</td><td>e</td><td>n</td><td>t</td><td>i</td><td>h</td><td>o</td><td>c</td><td>k</td><td>s</td><td>s</td><td>t</td></tr>
<tr><td>i</td><td>p</td><td>s</td><td>d</td><td>e</td><td>s</td><td>c</td><td>e</td><td>n</td><td>t</td><td>m</td><td>f</td><td>l</td><td>o</td></tr>
<tr><td>s</td><td>i</td><td>r</td><td>d</td><td>a</td><td>f</td><td>l</td><td>a</td><td>l</td><td>l</td><td>o</td><td>w</td><td>e</td><td>d</td></tr>
<tr><td>l</td><td>e</td><td>e</td><td>m</td><td>t</td><td>a</td><td>g</td><td>r</td><td>t</td><td>u</td><td>r</td><td>n</td><td>a</td><td>e</td></tr>
<tr><td>e</td><td>g</td><td>b</td><td>e</td><td>b</td><td>r</td><td>i</td><td>d</td><td>a</td><td>l</td><td>n</td><td>b</td><td>d</td><td>f</td></tr>
<tr><td>g</td><td>u</td><td>e</td><td>s</td><td>t</td><td>i</td><td>l</td><td>o</td><td>m</td><td>a</td><td>i</td><td>r</td><td>g</td><td>f</td></tr>
<tr><td>f</td><td>e</td><td>a</td><td>g</td><td>r</td><td>o</td><td>o</td><td>i</td><td>d</td><td>e</td><td>n</td><td>i</td><td>u</td><td>e</td></tr>
<tr><td>f</td><td>a</td><td>r</td><td>t</td><td>h</td><td>e</td><td>r</td><td>l</td><td>f</td><td>m</td><td>g</td><td>m</td><td>e</td><td>c</td></tr>
<tr><td>t</td><td>r</td><td>g</td><td>o</td><td>l</td><td>a</td><td>r</td><td>p</td><td>e</td><td>n</td><td>a</td><td>l</td><td>r</td><td>t</td></tr>
</table>
</td></tr>
<tr><td></td><td>3</td><td>Children's own answers.</td></tr>
<tr><td>18</td><td>1</td><td>Across: 1. principle, 5. father, 6. precede, 9. alter, 10. guessed, 12. farther, 14. lead, 16. desert, 17. stationery
Down: 1. passed, 2. compliment, 3. prophet, 4. effect, 7. descent, 8. affect, 9. allowed, 10. guest, 11. profit, 13. heard, 15. draught</td></tr>
<tr><td>19</td><td>2</td><td>Children's own answers, selecting words that are more interesting while in keeping with the story.</td></tr>
</table>

Page number	Question number	Answers
20	2	Children should underline these sentences: • This is to improve road safety by eliminating impersonation at driving tests and ensuring the person driving a vehicle is qualified to do so. • You may also find that other organisations, such as car hire firms and insurance companies, will ask to see both parts. • Drivers will need to renew their photocard licence every ten years until age 70 to keep the photograph up to date. • Drivers who are required to renew their licence at shorter intervals, for example, for medical reasons, or because they hold entitlement to drive buses or lorries, will not be required to renew their photograph at each renewal.
	3	Children should underline these sentences with wavy lines: • You will be issued with: • You must produce both the photocard and counterpart if requested by the police or a court. • You should also present both parts when taking a driving test.
	4	Children should circle most of these formal/subject-specific words: photocard, eliminating, impersonation, ensuring, vehicle, qualified, categories, entitled, counterpart, endorsements, provisional, entitlement, requested, validity, required, intervals Some variation in responses is fine but children should show an understanding of words that are in a formal register or are specific to the topic of the text.
21	2	Children's own answers. Children should write in complete, grammatical sentences and show some awareness of formal vocabulary choices.
22	2	Children's own answers.
23	1a	Children's own answers.
	1b	Children's own answers.
	1c	Children's own answers.
	1d	Children's own answers.
	1e	Children's own answers.
	1f	Children's own answers.
24	1	Children's own answers.
	2	Children's own answers.
25	1	reunify, categorise, solidify, facilitate, advertise, originate For this style of question, refer to a dictionary for the answers.
26	1	connect + dis = disconnect behave + mis = misbehave approve + dis = disapprove hear + mis = mishear clutter + de = declutter understand + mis = misunderstand like + dis = dislike throne + de = dethrone obey + dis = disobey mystify + de = demystify
	2a	deactivated
	2b	disapproves
	2c	misaddressed
	2d	disbelieved
	2e	distrusted
27	1a	past perfect
	1b	present perfect
	1c	past perfect
	1d	present perfect
	1e	past perfect
	2a	I had spent all morning tidying my bedroom.
	2b	Sam had looked everywhere for his pen.
	2c	Ellie had gone to the shops to get some sweets.
28	1	The following words should be underlined: can, will, would, could, should, may, might, can, ought, must, shall
	2	will/may/might, would/should, will/must/should/could/may/might, can, should/must/ought to, will
29	3	**Definite:** surely, definitely, certainly **Possible:** probably, maybe, perhaps, possibly
	4a	I can definitely go to judo next week.
	4b	Children's own answers using appropriate verbs.
	4c	Children's own answers using appropriate verbs.
	4d	Children's own answers using appropriate verbs.
	5a	I may possibly do my homework before bedtime.
	5b	Children's own answers using appropriate verbs.
	5c	Children's own answers using appropriate verbs.
30	1	that, who, whose, which/that, that, who, where, which/that, when, whose, that/which, where
31	1	Dad suddenly realised he was wearing odd socks, which he found very embarrassing. Janie walked down the street where the famous actor lived. Greg is the boy whose shoes got lost. I ate the sandwich which Mum made for me. The mouse disappeared into a tiny hole, which annoyed the cat. My favourite city is Dublin, which has many beautiful buildings. Mrs Baxter introduced the girl who was coming to join our class. I was getting out of the shower at the very moment when you knocked at the door. This is the famous athlete who won the marathon. I was ill on Wednesday, which meant I missed the play.
32	1	The following words should be underlined: Because, Firstly, and then, because, However, so, instead, When, finally, Then, Next, always, this, When, Unfortunately, just at that moment, Before, and, but, that, and then
33	2	Children's own answers.
34	1	Children's own answers, but arguments should be grouped roughly as follows: **For:** Zoos have saved many animals from extinction. Zoos allow people to see animals they would never see otherwise. It means people can observe them and learn about them. The animals have a safer life in the zoo than in the wild. They provide entertainment for people. It means more people are interested in the animals. **Against:** Zoos are unfair to animals. The animals change in captivity – sometimes they become neurotic. They confine animals in small spaces. Zoos don't give animals a natural life. Zoos cost too much and people can't afford to go to them. People can see these animals living in the wild on television, they don't need to go to a zoo.
35	2	Children's own answers.

Page number	Question number	Answers
36	1	The dogs, who had rolled about in the mud, were given baths. Grandmas, who like playing with their grandchildren, have lots of fun. The boys, who broke the window, were told off. The flowers, which were my mum's pride and joy, got squashed.
	2a	I finished my cake, sadly.
	2b	Let's eat James!
	2c	Don't stop!
	2d	As I was eating, the table collapsed.
	2e	While Mum was cooking, the baby started crying.
37	3a	The soldiers, who had been injured in battle, were taken to the hospital.
	3b	Trombones, which make a very loud noise, have been banned from the school orchestra.
	3c	The runners, who were on the uphill stretch of the race, were puffed out.
	3d	My favourite breakfast, which consists of cornflakes, toast, orange juice and porridge, was waiting for me when I came downstairs.
	3e	The teachers, who are often annoyed with me, were waiting for me to come in after lunch.
	3f	On my birthday, which comes just before Christmas, I received a new computer game, a pair of headphones, a book and two pairs of socks as presents.
	3g	The sharks, which had injured fins, swam slowly round and round.
	3h	Outside the shops, which are currently closed for refurbishment, I met Jamie, Alisha and Ben.
38	1	The tower, a tall building without any steps, was Rapunzel's home. An old woman, to whom the tower belonged, kept her a prisoner. She would shout, her voice croaking cruelly, "Rapunzel, let down your hair!" Rapunzel's hair, like a long ladder, hung down from the window. The old woman, who was more agile than she looked, scrambled up Rapunzel's hair. A handsome prince, who was hiding nearby, saw everything that happened.
	2	Children's own answers.
39	1a	Children's own answers, along these lines: The ducks, swimming serenely on the pond, were suddenly disturbed by a loud noise.
	1b	My uncle Sam (whose middle name is Albert) loves karaoke.
	1c	The Second World War (which took place between 1939 and 1945) was a time of great hardship for many people. (Commas could also be used in this sentence.)
	1d	I was sitting quietly in the kitchen when suddenly – crash bang wallop – I heard a terrible noise from overhead.
	1e	I love Saturdays (which always seem to take forever to come) because that is the day when I go to see Gran and Grandpa.
	1f	Suddenly the door was flung open – knocking my little sister flying – and a huge giant shouldered his way into the room.

Page number	Question number	Answers
40	1a	The wizard threw a lot of disgusting things into the cauldron: snakes' tongues, grasshoppers' legs, mud and rotten tomatoes.
	1b	My favourite hobbies are football, street dance, trampolining and sleeping.
	1c	There are a lot of children in my family: four brothers, two sisters and fourteen cousins.
	1d	There was a long queue ahead of us at the vet's: three cats, two dogs, a rabbit and four guinea pigs.
	2	Children's own answers.
41	1a	Around 100-odd people went to the school concert.
	1b	Jamie's dad is a used-car salesman.
	1c	Al Capone was a well-known gangster.
	1d	In winter I like to wear a fleece-lined coat.
	1e	The top-earning film this year was *Delilah Duck's Day Out*.
	1f	The band One Convention released this year's best-selling album.
	1g	I found a half-eaten chocolate bar at the bottom of my bag.
	2	Children's own answers.
42	1	Here are some rules for looking after your pet rabbits. • Give them space to hop about freely. • Make sure they have plenty of fresh water. • Offer them lots of green, leafy vegetables. Equipment you might need for your rabbits includes: • bowls for food and water • a hutch • a brush, if your rabbits have long fur.
44	1	Midnight
	2	Living people, laughing
	3	Seventh
	4	He was the driver of the hearse.
	5	Levi's Jeanswear, Adidas Sportswear and cosmetics
	6	Her sleep was restless and unsettled. Evidence: she wrestled with the duvet and thumped the pillow.
	7	The author indicates an unexplained noise on the driveway. Or because the sound is described so vividly, the reader feels involved.
	8	The effect is that the reader reads the sentence quickly and this builds up the tension and suspense of the scene.
	9	Peeped between the curtains Pulled the duvet up over her head She heard the gravel in the driveway crunch
	10	Children's own answers, giving reasons supported by the text to help justify their opinion.
46	1	Coal was a very important source of power to heat homes and run machinery.
	2	12 hours
	3	This was their day off.
	4	The belts needed to be big and strong because they were attached to chains that the hurriers used to pull the carts.
	5	Because the passages and doors were only about 66 centimetres high, which is much shorter than an average adult.
	6	Children's own answers, giving evidence from the text.
	7	Two of the following: miners often had accidents, the work was very tiring and difficult, the conditions were very bad for miners' health
	8	Because people were becoming more and more concerned about the conditions in which children were working, and felt the need to protect children from the dangers of working in a mine.

Page number	Question number	Answers
48	1	A suburban street corner
	2	A park
	3	He is waiting for Jamie to come so they can do something important, and he's worried Jamie may not turn up.
	4	He probably feels embarrassed, and/or worried that Mrs Turner will hang around and find out what he and Jamie are up to. You can tell this because of his hesitant language (Oh ... er ... hi, Mrs Turner) and the way he tries to quickly persuade her that everything is fine so that she'll go.
	5	Calm and laidback. Evidence includes speech such as You worry too much! and It'll be fine, you'll see.
	6	Accept any words in keeping with Cameron's personality in the play script, such as: anxious, nervous, worried, unsure
	7	Because they need to get to the park before the others.
	8	Ben and Jamal
	9	Accept any ideas that are plausible in the context of the play script. Children should pick up that the hidden thing must be something valuable or important and also secret.
	10	Accept any dialogue that plausibly supports the situation described in the question. More confident children may manage to write dialogue that reflects what they already know of Cameron's and Jamie's characters.
50	1	Children's own answers, but they pick up that the alternating italic and normal text helps to show that there are two different narrators in the poem.
	2	He says that his dad has to look at his watch to work out if it is day or night.
	3	a
	4	funny and cheeky
	5	He says that when his dad counts sheep, it's the sheep that go to sleep.
	6	Children's own answers, but they should pick up that both narrators speak in the last verse, and the structure is different because it's not about giving reasons why each dad is the worst.
	7	Children's own answers.
	8	Children's own answers.
51	1	

Text	Audience	Purpose	Features
Come to beautiful Balton! Enjoy the glorious sunshine on our secluded beach! Why wait to begin your dream holiday?	People who might be interested in buying a holiday.	To persuade people to buy a holiday.	Imperative language (*Come!*), exaggerated language (*glorious, secluded*), rhetorical question (*Why wait ...?*).
Mr Twinkletoes was a tiny elf. He lived all alone at the bottom of Martha's garden. Martha's mummy didn't know he existed, but Martha and the elf were best friends.	Young children.	To entertain.	Vocabulary (mummy) and ideas (tiny mythical creatures) appealing to the age group, simple sentence structures.
Hedgehogs and porcupines share some important characteristics. For example, they both have spines, or quills.	People of any age who want to learn about these animals.	To instruct.	Formal and subject-specific language (characteristics, quills, respects).

52	1	Children's own answers. Children should fill the spider diagram boxes appropriately bearing in mind the purpose (to inform and persuade), the audience (primary-aged children) and the features of the text type (persuasive leaflet).
53	2	Children's own answers. Children's writing should pick up on points from their spider diagram and from the prompts on the page, and be suitable for the identified purpose and audience.

Page number	Question number	Answers
54	1	Children's own answers. If there is an opportunity to discuss the activity, you could ask children to explain why they made their choice.
55	2	Children's own answers.
	3	Children's own answers. Should include an attempt to convey atmosphere by describing sounds. Some children may be able to add extra atmosphere by drawing on the other senses.
56	1a	a/c Accept other sensible answers.
	1b	a/b/c Accept other sensible answers.
	1c	a/b/c/d Accept other sensible answers.
	2	Children's own answers.
57	3	Children's own answers.
	4	Children's own answers.
	5	Children's own answers.
59	1	Children's own answers, which should draw on information from the timeline and use some cohesive words and phrases to link ideas.